Memorials of Scotland

By Gregor Stewart

Scottish Paranormal Book 3

Publishing

Scotland

www.beul-aithris-publishing.com

Copyright 2019 © Gregor Stewart

First Edition

ISBN 9781709583315

Contents

About the Author

Growing up in the town of St Andrews in Fife, with the ancient ruins of the castle and cathedral being my 'playgrounds' as a child, it was almost inevitable that I would develop a keen interest in Scottish history. My grandfather was a gold leaf expert which led him to work on the restoration of many prestigious buildings such as Falkland Palace and St Leonards Chapel, and tales he used to bring home that he had gathered from the staff at these locations only aided in fuelling my interest and imagination.

As a teenager, I had access to the libraries of the University of St Andrews to carry out some of my studies. With a vast collection of books, some centuries old, covering every topic imaginable, while I was meant to be carrying out research for my geography exam, instead I was sitting reading historical books covering the times of the Scottish witch trials. The beliefs and the brutality both fascinated and horrified in equal measures, and I was hooked on the darker and hidden side of history.

I first started writing this book around 10 years ago, after seeing a photo of the Maggie Wall monument and reading about the mystery that surrounds it. At the time it did not, however, feel right, and so the project was shelved. Since then I have written a number of paranormal books, a natural progression from the area of history I focus on, and historical books, which cover the forgotten stories of specific towns, including the witch trials for each area. With the additional research over that decade, the time felt right to return to this book and, rather than picking up where I had left off, I opted for a complete re-write.

I do hope I have shown the unfortunate women, and men, who are covered in the following pages the respect they deserved for their unimaginable treatment on the basis of nothing but hearsay, yet it is also important to remember that, difficult as it is to imagine, in these deeply suspicious times, many people thought they were doing the right thing, which I will cover in the introduction. Photographs throughout this book have in many instances come from my personal collection, have been contributed by associates or sourced from the websites Flickr and Geograph, and reproduced here under a creative commons license.

Introduction

Looking back at the times of the witch trials, it can be difficult for us to comprehend how such barbarity and cruelty could be inflicted on so many innocent people. While those who suffered were predominantly women, men and even children also underwent the horror of accusations, and the process to obtain a confession. However, it is important to remember that the fear of black magic and witchcraft was very real, and many of those involved genuinely believed they were dealing with real witches and were doing what was necessary to safeguard themselves.

The reason for this belief was the levels it came from. The Church at the time held great power, the ministers were both worshipped as pillars of the community, yet feared for their ability to issue harsh treatment for those who were not seen to respect the Word of God. When ordinary townsfolk were seeing crops failing, great storms damaging fishing fleets and unknown illnesses sweeping the towns and villages, and hearing not only their ministers but the hierarchy of the Church warning that the Devil was in their midst, it becomes clearer why people were willing to believe something supernatural was going on, and the wild accusations made against those who, for whatever reason, did not fit in. When the monarchy, the highest power in the land, also started to make accusations of witchcraft, this did nothing but cement the belief that anyone could fall under the power of the Devil, and carry out his deeds, and it was the Witchcraft Act of 1563 that would start a truly devastating time in the country's history.

Mary, Queen of Scots, was responsible for this Witchcraft Act, and there is speculation on her reasons for introducing such a savage piece of legislation. At the time of her reign, Scotland was in turmoil. The country had been devoutly Catholic for over 1000 years, and St Andrews was considered to be Scotland's Rome. Yet while Mary had been in exile and raised under the Catholic faith in France, the Protestant Reformation had arrived in her native Scotland. The changes had not been easy, with essentially civil war breaking out as supporters of the opposing faiths fought for control. By the time Mary returned to take her rightful place as Queen of Scotland, the country had largely converted, and the power of the Catholic Church was fading. With England also already being a Protestant country, the links between the two former enemies were growing, while the alliance with Catholic France, was weakening. Queen Mary eventually had no option but to make an uneasy truce with the leaders of the Protestant Church in Scotland, despite not converting herself, something that would cause obstacles and distrust throughout her reign.

Although Scotland had largely converted, there were still pockets of the 'old faiths' that remained across the country: Cunning Folk who knew the healing properties of plants could prepare potions and medicines for people in the need of help, and it was perhaps a desire to put and end to this which inspired Queen Mary to introduce her Witchcraft Act.

The Protestant faith was also considered by many to be less restrictive and had given women a new feeling of optimism. Yet the Witchcraft Act would discourage any woman from acting out of the ordinary or to stand out from the crowd, for fear of getting the finger pointed at them. Perhaps Queen Mary hoped this would start a reversal in the country, back to the Catholic faith where there had been a feeling of security under the protection of the Church, yet her real reasons can only be speculated upon. The Act initially only saw the condemnation of the old herbalists, who were made an example of and persecuted to try to force all to turn to Christianity. Queen Mary did not live long enough to see the true effects of her law, as it was not until events that took place around the wedding of her son, King James VI and I, brought true witch-mania to Scotland.

In 1589, King James was married to Anne of Denmark in Copenhagen at a proxy wedding, meaning neither were actually present at the time, after which the new Queen was to set sail for Scotland to be united with her husband. Her fleet was soon met with sudden and violent storms, forcing them to seek shelter in Norway. After several failed attempts, King James decided to take his own fleet from Scotland, and sail out to collect his Queen. In November 1589, the couple were formally married at the Bishop's Palace in Oslo, before returning to Denmark to have a celebratory tour. At the time, the belief in witchcraft was far stronger in mainland Europe than it had been in Scotland, largely due to a book written in 1486 by Heinrich Kramer and Jacob Sprenger titled the *Malleus Maleficarum*, meaning the Hammer of Witches in Latin. First published in Germany in 1487, the book was basically an instruction manual on the reasons women would turn to witchcraft, how to find evidence of this, and ultimately how to put those convicted of witchcraft to death. King James was a theologist, and with Denmark being in the grips of a perceived witch epidemic at the time of his tour, he took great interest in the belief system, and the writings of the *Malleus Maleficarum*.

By the time the Royal couple were ready to set sail for Scotland in May 1590, he had learned much about the witchcraft, and the associated risks, a knowledge he was soon to put to use. Just as Queen Anne's earlier attempts to sail to Scotland had been hindered by storms, so too were the couple's return. It is said that storms rose from nowhere, forcing the ships back, and it took several attempts before the fleet finally made it back to Scotland. Needless to say, the Danish authorities who had prepared the fleet for the return journey faced embarrassment at failing to have the ships fully seaworthy, and a minister was accused of deliberately understocking the royal boat, making it unstable in the rough seas, yet there was a convenient excuse. He, in turn, blamed a local woman for causing the instability in the vessels by using witchcraft to replace full barrels with empty barrels, meaning no one knew until it was too late. A quite outrageous accusation today, yet in these deeply superstitious times, it was an accusation that was taken seriously. No doubt following horrific torture, the woman not only confessed to the crime, but named others who she claimed had worked with her to try to not only sink the Queen's ship on her initial failed attempts to reach Scotland, but to also trying to sink the royal couple's boat. Included amongst those charged was a woman named Anna Koldings, better known by the nickname the Mother of the Devil, giving a clear indication that she was not a popular lady, and no doubt the trial was seen as a convenient way to rid the community of her. In total, 13 women were burned at the stake for using witchcraft to attempt to kill the King and Queen of Scotland.

When word reached King James that those responsible had not only been identified but dealt with through the Danish Justice system, he appears to have become curious as to whether the Danish witches may have been working with others closer to home. What followed became known as the North Berwick Witch Trials, a two-year legal case, which would lead to the death of around 70 men and women, all of whom had been accused and convicted of using witchcraft to try to kill the monarchy. As part of his ongoing learning of the interrogation methods for accused witches, King James sat in personally on several of these sessions, including torture, before publishing his own book on the matter, titled *Daemonologie*, in 1597. If witchcraft had not been seen as real by the common people before, hearing of their King not only overseeing a massive trial, but writing a book on the matter, would have been sure to quell any doubts, and to dispute the existence of witchcraft would mean not only going against the word of the Church, but against the monarchy.

Just as many believed Queen Mary's initial intentions had been, suspicion and blame quickly fell on anyone who did not quite fit in. People quickly fell into line, once again turning to the Church, albeit now the Protestant Church, for protection, raising the importance and rule of the Church once more. Many communities were walled, and few ventured outwith their own towns, so when natural disasters such as the crop failures happened, the finger of blame was quickly pointed either at any visitors to the area, or anyone who had acted in a manner not expected of them. In some instances, it also provided a convenient way to rid the towns of the elderly, who were no longer making a meaningful contribution and were becoming a burden. Even a fossil known as a gryphaea, formed from an extinct species of oyster and once relatively common on the beaches of Scotland, was seen as evidence the Devil was in the local area due to its likeness to a claw.

To be accused of witchcraft was very simple, yet devastating. Missing church was seen as a sin and raised suspicion, with minor things such as talking to an animal, something we all do today, could be used against you. Once accused, there was one aim, to prove your guilt by whatever means necessary, including torture. Initial methods such a sleep deprivation and a process known as 'walking the witch', which involved wrapping a rope painfully tight around the head, and using the opposite end as a lead to force the victim to walk continuously, were common. Devices such as the witches fork, a metal bar with two spikes that fit under the chin forcing the head backward, were used to prevent sleep outside of torture sessions. If no confession was being offered, more extreme methods would be put into practice, such as the thumbscrews, better known in Scotland as the Pilliwinks, to crush not only the thumbs but all the fingers and the toes. The booties, a large wooden or metal boot into which one or both feet could be placed were also used. The bootie came up to just below the knee, and metal or wooden wedges would be driven in with a hammer, slowly reducing the space inside and crushing the lower legs and ankles.

In extreme cases, a specialist witchfinder known as a witch pricker would be brought in. The belief was that once a witch had fallen under the control of Satan, he would remove their Christian baptism and replace it with one of his own. This identifying mark, which could be a simple mole or skin tag, was seen as evidence, yet for proof, it would have to be impervious to pain. The pricker got their name from the tools of their trade, long, sharp pins that they would push into these marks to see if any pain was felt. Of course, a skilled pricker could spend hours working round a body, eventually using the pin to numb the area around a mark, which resulted in no pain being felt when the pin was driven in. Failure to find a suitable mark did not mean you were innocent, it just meant the mark may be within your body, resulting in large areas being 'pricked' seeking the unseen mark under the skin.

It is little wonder that many simply confessed, as being accused really was a hopeless situation. No help could be offered by friends or even family due to the following wording from the 1563 Witchcraft Act, which can be found in multiple sources:

Nor that na persoun seik ony help, response or cosultatioun at ony sic usaris or abusaris foirsaidis of Witchcraftis, Sorsareis or Necromancie, under the pane of deid, alsweill

to be execute aganis the usar, abusar, as the
seikar of the response or consultatioun.

As a rough translation, this wording rules that anyone who was seen to assist, consult with or help a witch, would be deemed a witch themselves and also executed. All that a loved one could do was turn to the Church and pray for their salvation. It really was a terrifying time for those who lived through it and a very sad time for us to reflect back upon.

By the time the Witchcraft Acts were repealed in 1736, an estimated 4000 innocent men, women and children had been sent to their deaths. Many of the records of the witch trials have either been lost or were simply not documented in the first place as they were not deemed important enough. Yet momentum is growing for this tragic time to be remembered with a national memorial to commemorate those who perished. While this may be some time off, there are a number of markers and smaller monuments across the country to remember local trials, and throughout this book, I will look at many of these, and explore the story behind them.

The old Kirk at North Berwick, where it was claimed the witches would meet

The Witches Well, Edinburgh

The start of the North Berwick Witch Trials can be traced back to a lady named Geillis Duncan, a housemaid in the employment of Chamberlain David Seton, a wealthy man who resided in Tranent, just outside Edinburgh. He had observed that Geillis was leaving the house at night and, under the cover of darkness, she was meeting with locals to provide care for the ill. What was nothing other than a good deed, was sufficient for Geillis to fall under the suspicion of being a witch, and her employer reported his concerns to the authorities.

Upon hearing her story, she was accused of using supernatural powers given to her by the Devil to heal the sick, rather than have them seek the divine intervention of God, as was expected at the time. Poor Geillis underwent horrific torture, including the thumbscrews, yet would not confess to using witchcraft. The identification of marks, believed to be the Devils Marks, were however seen as enough proof of her guilt and she was thrown in prison, where she underwent further intense torture.

Documents from the time describe the intention of the torture and interrogation process to be to make the accused life feel like a burden to them. In other words, to put them in a position where they would prefer to die than continue living as they were. As was the case in most trials, these methods were successful with Geillis, who eventually broke and confessed. There is little doubt that she was fed information to confess to, as it was exactly what was being sought at the time. She told that she was a member of a witches coven comprising of around 200 witches, who were acting on behalf of the Earl of Bothwell, one of King James's greatest foes. She told that on the evening of Halloween, 1590, as the King's fleet was entering the Firth of Forth having finally made the voyage from Denmark, the witches gathered at St Andrews Old Kirk in North Berwick, where they listened to a sermon delivered by the Devil himself. She went on to provide a list of around 70 names of fellow witches who were present at the time.

King James took a personal interest in the trial, although it is likely his advisors had already directed the proceedings to ensure that would be the case, knwing that having the Earl of Bothwell named would draw his attention. The King had all of those named brought in for questioning, while Geillis was burned at the stake at the Castle Esplanade in Edinburgh. As well as the Earl of Bothwell, a number of other prominent local people were implicated, with the leader being named as Dr. John (also recorded as James) Fian, a local schoolmaster who was said to also be a powerful wizard. Clearly a well-educated man, Dr. Fian refused to confess to the crimes of which he was accused. He underwent the most unimaginable torture including sleep deprivation, having his fingers crushed in thumbscrews and his legs being crushed in the booties. He is also said to have had his fingernails pulled out with crude pliers and pins driven into the bare, exposed flesh, yet still, he would not break. Instead of considering the possibility that he was innocent, the authorities decided he was to be made an example of for his resistance, and he was stretched on the Rack. A confession was eventually obtained, although it is disputed whether this was under worsening, undocumented torture, or whether it was trickery to have him sign documentation in his weakened state, not realising what it was.

In his confession, he stated he had been present at all of the meetings of the witches coven, and took pledges of allegiance to the Devil from the women, presenting them directly to the Dark Lord. He also stated he used magic to win the hearts of local women for his own pleasure and that he carried a moles foot which was the source of his power. The confession was no doubt used to justify the continued treatment, demonstrating to others that perseverance will break even the strongest of the witches, before he too was burned at the stake in front of Edinburgh Castle.

Some reports indicate that the extreme confessions were causing some doubt in the King's mind, although it is said it was the actions of a prominent midwife, Agnes Sampson, who was one of the accused that convinced the King. She requested to speak to him in private and passed a message to him, which was reputed to be a conversation that had taken place between his new bride and himself on the ship while travelling back from Denmark. It is likely details of this conversation were passed to Agnes, without the relevance of it being told to her, and she was tricked to passing it on to the King. It was, however, sufficient to convince him that he was under attack from witches, who even knew what was happening in his private life, and he had Agnes taken to the Palace of Holyrood House where he personally oversaw her torture, until the inevitable confession was obtained, and Agnes was sent to be burned at the stake at Edinburgh Castle.

The information gathered from the collective confessions were that, under the guidance of the Devil, the witches had dug up bodies from across the Kirkyard and removed specific body parts and organs. These were all attached to a dead cat before it was thrown into the sea to conjure up a massive storm to attempt to sink the King's fleet as it entered the Firth of Forth. It was said that the Devil had instructed the witches to do so, as with his new knowledge, the returning King was their greatest enemy in the world. Although exact numbers, nor details of all of the individual confessions are not available, it is likely that all 70 people named by Geillis met their death at the Castle Esplanade in Edinburgh, with the only saving grace being that most were strangled to death before the flames were lit. The Earl of Bothwell himself was eventually put to trial in 1593, yet a sign of his power and influence, even a charge of wrongdoing against the King was not sufficient, and he was found not guilty.

At the Castle Esplanade, an inconspicuous cast-iron fountain can be found on the wall of the Tartan Weaving Mill and Experience building. The fountain was originally used as a drinking well, but unfortunately no longer operates. The building to which it is attached used to house one of the cities reservoirs, but in 1992 when the reservoir was no longer used, the fountain ceased operating. Cast in 1894, and designed by John Duncan. The Witches Well, as it is known, is a memorial not just to the North Berwick witches, but to the hundreds of innocent people burned at the Esplanade for the crime of witchcraft, and contains a number of symbols relevant to that time. A series of 'witches' heads, with a snake weaving around, is to show the fine balance between wisdom and evil, and plants, including the foxglove which could heal and also harm depending on the dosage, the God of Medicine and the Goddess of Health are incorporated to symbolise the many herbal healers who perished for their profession. The years 1479 and 1722 are shown in Roman Numerals, giving the dates between which the witch trials took place, and the Wiccan symbols for air and water are also included.

The water trough extends out so has three sides, with the front depicting a floral display, one side showing the evil eye and the other side showing hands holding a bowl, to symbolise healing. A plaque later added reads:

This fountain designed by John Duncan RSA is near the site on which many witches were burned at the stake. The wicked head and serene head signify that some used their exceptional knowledge for evil purposes while others were misunderstood and wished their kind nothing but good. The Serpent has the dual significance of Evil and of Wisdom. The Foxglove spray further emphasises the dual purpose of many common objects.

The Witches Well, Edinburgh

Grissel Jaffray, Dundee

As with many towns and cities, there are virtually no records of there being any witch trials held in Dundee. And there may be a very good reason for this: witch trials were expensive, as shown in the following invoice from a case held in Kirkcaldy, which can be sourced widely in many publications:

Expense incurred for the Judge: 6 Shillings

Payment to the executioner for his pains: 8 pounds, 14 shillings

Executioner's expenses: 16 shillings, 4 pennies

Hemp coats: 3 pounds 10 shillings

Making of the above : 8 shillings

Hangman's Rope: 6 shillings

Tar Barrel: 14 Shillings

10 loads of coal: 3 pounds, 6 shillings and 8 pennies.

While the family of the accused may have been responsible to pay the charges where they could, in many cases it fell upon the town itself to meet the costs and so, an outbreak of witchcraft could prove a very costly time for the authorities. As is commonly the case, the information from the Dundee witch trials can, however, be pieced together from other documents, where brief mentions are made of the cases. In 1888 book, *The Annals of an Angus Parish*, by Rev. W. Mason Inglis, reference is made that on 27th April 1669, an action was ordered by the Presbytery of Dundee to oblige the authorities of Dundee to force anyone who it was even suggested may be connected with witchcraft to move out of the town, a ruling that ensured that Dundee would have minimal involvement with witch trials by making those likely to be accused another town's problem.

That is not to say Dundee had no witch trials. A study of historic maps reveals locations such as 'Witches Knowe' a name commonly given to elevated pieces of land where executions often took place. In Dundee, this was in the Hawkhill area of the City, although at the time it was outside the town boundary, again an indication of the lands former use as fear of spirits returning from the dead would often result in executions occurring out with the town walls. A small loch close to Witches Knowe was likely to have been used for the practice of 'dooking the witch', the process of throwing the bound accused into the water to see if they floated or sunk.

As water was believed to be pure, it would accept the body if it too was pure, but if it was not pure, the water would reject the body, pushing them to the surface which was deemed sufficient proof for the accused to be executed. A further mound around Guthrie Street in the city is believed to have also been used to execute accused witches.

The 1845 book, *The History of Dundee: From the Earliest to the Present Time* makes mention of an entry in the diary of the Earl of Moray stopping in Dundee while on business on behalf of King James VI, to watch a company of witches being burned at the stake. How many there were is not noted, however, it must have been more than one.

While there are some other recorded cases of 'low level' witchcraft, known as charming, which was used, for example, to alleviate illnesses, these did not bring the true weight of the Witchcraft Act down on the accused. It is the trial of a woman named Grissell Jaffray which is best known in the city. Not due to records of the trial, as any documentation that did exist was mysteriously destroyed, along with other town papers from the time, but thanks to the discovery in 1815 of an extract from the town council's minutes which gives some details, and gives starting points to research her story, which starts with details of her husband, Robert Butchart.

Although his exact date of birth is not known, he was born into an influential Dundee family in the 1590s. His family had run a successful bakers business for several generations, and in 1615 he was recognised by being made a burgess, and possibly extending the business to open the first brewery in Dundee. Grissell similarly came from a wealthy family, believed to have been merchants, from Aberdeen, and although the date of their wedding is not known, they are recorded as living together as husband and wife in a house on Calendar Close, a small courtyard development which has long been lost and which sat beneath the current Overgate Shopping Centre in the city.

Exactly what Grissell did to draw attention to her is not documented. However, she was an outsider and being from a successful family, she is likely to have a degree of confidence which would make her stand out. She was also well educated and sharing that knowledge would be enough to cause suspicion. The most likely reason, however, is that her family is believed to have been Quakers, a religious movement established in 1650 that challenged the ideology of the authorities, leading to those who followed the faith to be persecuted. Grissell may have tried to introduce the Quaker belief system to Dundee, something sure to make her a prime target.

It was not until 11th November 1669, that Grissell was finally charged with witchcraft, by which time she would have been quite elderly. She was held in the Tollbooth in Dundee before facing trial, and although again no records exist of accusations or interrogation, it is recorded that the trial was led by John Kinloch, Dean of Guild, and John Tarbert, Provost of Dundee, confirming it did go ahead. She is recorded as being found guilty 'due to the mark', a clear indication that her ordeal went all the way through the process to that of having to use the services of a witch pricker. Just twelve days after being charged, on 23rd November 1669, Grissell was burned at the stake in the Seagate area of the city, close to the docks.

The execution of Grissell had a devastating effect on her family. Her husband's fortunes were lost, and he is later recorded as applying for admittance to the city's hospital, which did not refer to a medical facility as we would think today, but was a poor house for the destitute. It is also said that she had a son who had become a successful merchant in the city, who had the misfortune of returning to Dundee at the time of the execution. Having been travelling, he had no idea of the situation, yet had seen the smoke rise from the Seagate as his ship sailed into the dock. Upon landing, he asked what had been burning, no doubt fearing that a warehouse or similar may have been damaged, but was instead stunned to be told it had been his mother. Upon hearing what had happened, he is said to have returned to his ship and set sail once again, never returning to Dundee, and so ending the once prominent family connection to the city. This part of the story was immortalised in a poem named *The Witch-Wife's Son*.

Although Grissell is often said to have been the last witch burned in Dundee, minutes taken from the authority's meetings state that in February 1670, a 'prover', another name for a witchfinder, was employed in the city.

A memorial to Grissell can be found in Peter Street in the city centre, close to the spot where she perished, and consist of a mosaic in the pavement depicting the flames in which she was burned, and a plaque on the wall giving brief details of her tale. Sadly, this is very much overlooked, with thousands of people passing every week, with no knowledge of what the marker symbolises.

The Mosaic commemorating Grissel Jaffray

Lilias Adie, Torryburn

While towns such as Dundee and Stirling turned their backs on witch trials due to the expense, the authories of Dunfermline, Fife positively embraced them. This is possibly due to the town being home of one of the main Royal palaces of the time, and there was an element of willingness within the town authorities to be seen to carry out the wishes of the monarchy, whatever the cost.

The town boasts one of the earliest witch trials, conducted not long after the introduction of Queen Mary's Witchcraft Act. A local lady named Bessie Boswell, better known as Auld Bessie Bittern, meaning Old Bitter Bessie, was well known as someone not to be crossed, as her nickname would suggest. As someone who was unlikely to abide by rules she did not agree with, she was exactly the type of person the Witchcraft Act was introduced to deal with. She was often seen with a large, black cat that she would speak to, and she was said to mutter curses under her breath to anyone who she disagreed with. It was inevitable that as the fear of witchcraft grew, Bessie would fall under suspicion.

It is said that she had approached a local weaver, named Johnnie, to ask if he would be able to dig some potatoes for her from her garden the following morning. While Johnnie seemed quite amenable to the request, his wife overheard the conversation and explained to Bessie that he did not have time as he still had a lot of cloth to weave for an order that was due. Bessie clearly objected to this interference and warned his wife that not digging her potatoes will not allow him get the cloth made any quicker. An argument followed, and Bessie went on to say that refusing to dig the potatoes will make them no richer, and stormed out.

The following day, the meaning of Bessie's words became clear. As Johnnie returned to his loom to finish weaving the cloth to fulfill the order, every time he tried to start, the shuttle would fly from his hand. He repeatedly picked it up and tried to start again, but every time it would fly from his grip. Realising that Bessie's warning had been that until he dug the potatoes, he would neither be able to weave the cloth nor make any money from its sale, he feared that the shuttle had been cursed. In a desperate attempt to break the bewitchment, he took it to the kitchen and passed it through the flames of the fire three times. Whether this process, which must have been a local belief, worked or not is not documented, but Bessie was reported, arrested and charged with witchcraft, although for her crimes she was banished rather than be burned.

The religious reformation not only brought destruction to towns such as Dunfermline, with prominent Catholic religious establishments being attacked, but it also brought poverty, with many local businesses that had grown to serve these establishments suddenly finding their trade was gone. As the Reformation took grip, people, businesses and even whole towns who had relied on the Catholic Church for employment and trade, fell into poverty. Desperate people would take desperate action, and the towns misfortunes fuelled the allegations of the Devil being at work. As a result, the witch trials continued for a further century. Keen to lay the blame somewhere, it was claimed witches were operating in the area, yet it seemed some resistance remained. In 1614, the Earl of Dunfermline, Lord Chancellor of Scotland, intervened in one case with a ruling that the testimony of unqualified witnesses could not be heard in a trial. As a result, 14 of the witnesses could not be called and the case was dismissed. This was soon to change, as the move to not rely on witnesses and instead to force confessions became more common.

An initial outbreak of witchcraft in the town in 1627 was successfully dealt with, and when a further outbreak occurred in 1640, further action was taken. The town officials employed the services of an official town executioner named Pat Mayne, who went under the title of Hangman and Witch Burner. It was clear there was an intention to send the message out to the townsfolk that witchcraft was being taken seriously. Pat seemed to relish in his new role, becoming known as 'The Notorious' Pat Mayne. To aid in the town's pursuit of witches, Witch Watchers and Witch Catchers were later employed. The Watchers' sole task was to observe the daily activities in the town, watching for anyone acting out of character or unusually. Anyone who caught the attention of the watchers would be reported to the catchers, who were responsible for seizing and imprisoning the suspects, with an aim to bring them to trial. No one was above suspicion, yet the wealthy were able to buy their way out before being sent to trial thereby avoiding the clause of the Witchcraft Act that forbade anyone from assisting a witch and bringing much-needed money to the town authorities. For those not fortunate enough to pay, once their trial started they were facing almost certain death.

The area around the upper end of Townhill Road was formerly known as Witch Loan and led to the place of execution for those convicted of witchcraft at a small hill, identified on historic maps as Witch Knowe. Just to the north of this, the gallows stood for the execution of other criminals. A small body of water known as the Witch Pool remains in the garden grounds of a private house nearby, although the records show it was another pool a short distance away, known as Witches Dub, said to measure approximately 90 feet in diameter and between 6 and 10 feet deep, that was used for the dooking of the witches. This was filled in during the 18th century and nothing remains of it today.

In 1643, not long after the introduction of the Witch Watchers and Catchers, Dunfermline entered into a year long period of rounding up and burning accused witches. Many were simply the elderly, even walking with a staff was seen as an indication of practicing sorcery. Yet targeting the elderly was to prove to cause some problems for the authorities. On 20th June 1643, one of those accused named Jonett (Janet) Fentoun Marr, died in prison. Having been accused of witchcraft, to give her a Christian burial would have been unheard of, yet as she had not been convicted of the crime, she could not face the penalty of her body being burned. Instead, the records show that her body was unceremoniously dragged up Witch Loan to a waiting cart, which carried her the rest of the way to Witch Knowe where she was buried in an unmarked grave in the un-consecrated land.

Just a couple of months later, the authorities faced the same dilemma when another accused, Isobell Marr, hung herself in prison. The treatment of her body was the same, with her being buried at Witch Knowe. Other trials were however more successful, and over a three month period six women, Grissel Morris, Margaret Brand, Katherine Elder, Agnes Kirk, Margaret Donaldson, and Isobel Millar were successfully found guilty of witchcraft and burned at the stake at Witch Knowe, simply for not fitting into societies expectations.

It was the later trial of Lilias Adie, who lived in the village of Torryburn, around seven miles west from Dunfermline, that would be best remembered in the area. The town church was led by the Reverend Allan Logan, who had earned a reputation of being one of the most successful witch-finders in Scotland. It was said that during Sunday services, he would often stop and simply point towards the congregation, before shouting 'You, Witch! Rise and be gone from the table of the Lord'. As everyone sat wondering who he was pointing at, on almost every occasion at least one terrified woman would stand and leave, only to be arrested by Baillies waiting on the opposite side of the church door.

It was a neighbour of Lilias, named Jean Nelson, who made the accusations, claiming that Lilias had caused her ill health. She was taken to the church where she was to plead her innocence in front of the minister and elders before a decision was made as to how to proceed, yet clearly confused at what was happening and faced with such a notorious witchfinder, Lilias inadvertently confirmed the accusations made against her were true. She was then interrogated further, and with suggestions almost certainly being put to her as to what happened, she confirmed that she had been approached by a stranger in a cornfield, who later identified himself as the Devil.

Having fallen under his spell, she would then take other women to the same cornfield, luring them in using an unnatural blue light, so that they too would fall under the power of the Devil and do his bidding for him. Needless to say, with such a confession Lilias was charged and imprisoned in Dunfermline, yet as had happened before with the elderly accused, she died before being convicted. Her trial had been higher profile due to the levels of confessions she had made, and so it was not so easy for the authorities to simply dispose of her in an unmarked grave as they had done before.

With fear growing within the community, she was taken to the beach between Torryburn and Torrie, where she was buried in the sand at the tide line. There was the belief that due to the purity of the water, Lilias would be unable to rise through it, along with a belief that a witch could not cross moving water, and so the continuous movement of the tide would keep the spirit of Lilias contained and prevent her from seeking vengeance of the people of the town. For extra measures, a massive stone slab was also placed over her grave, to weigh the body down and prevent it from rising.

Sadly, her story does not end there. During the more liberal times of the 19th century, a rather morbid fascination with collecting relics of the witch trials became popular. With the location of the burial site of Lilias being documented, parts of her body were dug up and put up for sale to antiquarians. It is known her skull spent some time at St Andrews University, where it was studied, prior to being passed to a museum, but details of its whereabouts have since been lost. The studies did, however, confirm she was around 70 years old at the time of her death, and had very prominent buck teeth, something that would have made her stand out at the time, and could have led to the accusations being made against her.

In 2014, a renewed effort was made to once again locate the grave of Lilias Adie and a small group of professionals, led by Fife Council's archaeologist, Doug Spiers, set about trying to find the 'great stone doorstep' that was said to have identified its location. The pursuit was successful, with the prominent marker being once again uncovered to allow people to pay their respects to this unfortunate woman who found herself facing the most horrific treatment through no fault of her own. A campaign is currently underway to recover the parts of her body that were removed, including her skull, and for a more appropriate memorial for Lilias and the other Fife Witches to be remembered.

Fife Council Archaeologist, Doug Spiers uncovering Lilias Adie's Stone. Photo reproduced with kind permission of Fife Council Archaeological Department.

The Cluny Hill Witches, Forres

The historic town of Forres in Moray is a popular tourist destination today, and many enjoy walks through the forested area of Cluny Hill on the outskirts of the town, where Nelson's Tower can be found, erected in 1806 as a memorial to Admiral Lord Nelson. Yet it is it an often missed stone that stands at the bottom of the hill, ironically outside the Police station, that acts as a memorial of much darker times in the town.

It is near Forres that, in his famous play *Macbeth*, William Shakespeare has the title character meet the three witches, and this is possibly based on the tale of the Cluny Witches. Although documents to support the claims are somewhat scant, according to a long-term local legend three wise women lived on Cluny Hill during the reign of King Duncan 1 (1034 to 1040) and prophesied his downfall, in favour of a local ruler, Mac Bethad mac Findláich, better known as Macbeth. When King David invaded Morayshire in 1040, and met the forces of Macbeth outside Elgin, just over ten miles away from Cluny Hill, the King was slain in battle and Macbeth succeeded him as King of Scotland.

Macbeth ruled until 1057 when he was slain in battle by King David's son, Malcolm Canmore, who had been taken to England as a child for his own safety after the death of his father, yet had returned to take his rightful place as the Monarch. It is likely that it was after Malcolm was crowned King Malcolm III in 1058, that the unfortunate women of Cluny Hill met their grisly fate.

It is said that after being accused and convicted of witchcraft, they were forced into stout barrels at the top of Cluny Hill. The barrels had metal spikes driven into the sides all round before they were rolled down the hill, causing horrific injuries to the women inside. When the barrels stopped, they were set alight, burning the mangled remains of the victims, and you can only hope that they had already perished from their injuries. Large stones were placed where the barrels had been burned as a warning to others of the fate that they would face for practicing witchcraft.

Although only one stone is marked, three stones once existed marking the position where the three accused witches were burned. Of the three stones, two remain, with the unmarked stone being in a private garden closed to Victoria Road. The third stone was broken up in 1802 during roadworks, and at this time what is now known as the Witches Stone was also damaged and, having been broken into three pieces, it was incorporated into a house that was being built. It is said that those who lived there had nothing but bad luck, and local superstition led to the house being demolished, and the stone being repaired with large metal staples and returned to its rightful place. Others also make the connection of the stone having been broken into three to represent the three witches of Macbeth, although as mentioned there were originally three separate stones, and so this is unlikely.

There is some debate on the likelihood of this legend, and many believe that the memorials are from the more recent witch trials of the 17th and 18th centuries, and it was during this time that one of the most bizarre and surprising stories of the area comes. In 1662, a woman named Christian Caddell watched as an accused witch underwent torture at the hands of a Witch-Pricker trying to locate the Devil's mark. Instead of being horrified at the treatment of a fellow woman, Christian decided that she could do that herself!

Disguised as a man, and going under the name of John Patterson, Christian arrived in Moray at a time when the fear of witches was at its peak. The authorities in Elgin were taken in by her claims to be able to identify the witches in the local communities, and the Baillie of Spynie was first to sign her up to weed out the evil-doers. Such was her success, that her services were in much demand and she pursued witches as far away as Tain, north of Inverness, yet it was here that she would meet her downfall. She decided to put a local man named John Hay through the Pricking process, unaware that he was a court messenger with knowledge of the law. He petitioned for her arrest for wrongful accusations and, although successful, Christian had fled.

She soon found new work, dealing with a witchcraft accusation made against tenants of a highland croft by their landlord. Yet the tenants were MacLeans, and when word reached the Clan Chief, MacLean of Duart, he too petitioned the government, and this time she was arrested and taken to Edinburgh's notorious tollbooth. It was here that the shocking discovery that the infamous witch-pricker John Patterson, was, in fact, a woman, was made.

At her trial Christian claimed she had the ability to identify witches by looking into their eyes and she had used this, rather than the pricking process, to identify her victims. A risky move by all accounts, as such an ability could itself be seen as witchcraft. Yet whether it was to try to save the local authorities from further embarrassment, or for some other reason, Christian was sentenced to deportation to the Barbados Plantations, leaving on a boat on 4th May 1663, which is said to have been the same day that her final victim was burned at the stake in Forres.

It is thought Christian sent between six and ten women to the flames, and it would make anyone wonder why she would do such a thing during a time when women were so persecuted. Yet the motive was likely to be financial. The contracts she had secured were said to have paid six shillings a day, an average wage for a man and way above what a woman might have expected to earn, along with a massive bonus of six Scots Pounds for every witch identified.

The Witches Stone, Forres

Maxwellton Cross Memorial, Paisley

Events in 1696 in Paisley, just outside the city of Glasgow, would lead to one of the largest single witchcraft trials in the country.

In August of that year, Christian, the daughter of John Shaw, the Laird of Baragarran, witnessed one of the house servants, Catherine Campbell, take some milk from the kitchen and drink it. Something no one would consider out of the ordinary today, but then a servant would not be permitted to help themselves to anything, and it was considered theft. Christian told her mother what she had seen, which resulted in a severe berating for Catherine, something that she did not appreciate and she later angrily told 11-year-old Cristian that she hoped the Devil would haul her soul to Hell for telling her mother about the milk.

Just four days later, Christian had a brief encounter with a local woman named Agnes Naismith, who many claimed was a witch, and the next day Christian fell ill. Whether this illness was a coincidence, through fear from the words of Catherine Campbell followed by the encounter with an alleged witch, or simply malicious pretence, the timing raised concerns that witchcraft was at play. It is said that Christian began to have seizures and, with no improvement in Christian's health her family sought the help of various doctors, yet none of the treatment seemed to help. Over the following weeks and months, her condition seemed to get worse, with her complaining of great pains in her sides. Dr. Matthew Brisbane, a prominent physician from Glasgow, was contacted, and she was put under his care for ten days before being sent home, seemingly well again, but not long after her return, her illness struck again. During her seizures, her body would go stiff at times, described as being like a corpse, and the pains in her sides returned.

It was decided to take her back to Glasgow to receive further treatment from Dr. Brisbane, but on the way she had another seizure, following which she produced a ball of hair from her throat. It is said the hair was of different colours, some straight, some plaited, and in great quantities. She started coughing up more hair around every 15 minutes on her journey to Glasgow, and then for a further three days when under the care of Dr. Brisbane. After the third day, she began to produce coal from her mouth and, when Dr. Brisbane examined it, he found it to be hot to touch, with him judging it to be far hotter than the human body alone could have made it. This regurgitation of unusual items continued for two more days, with a quantity of straw said to contain pins and small animal bones amongst what was being brought up. Small candlesticks followed, and what appeared to be a leg bone from a bird, with the physicians' present claiming that as they were trying to pull these items from her throat, another force was trying to pull them back in. Over the coming days, more and more bizarre objects were being produced, including mouthfuls of feathers, bones, eggshells, and even stone gravel. Most notable, in between these seizures during which items were pulled from her mouth, Christian seemed in completely normal health.

After days of these incidents, during a seizure Christian was heard to call for a bible and a candle, although she seemed to be in a trance. She continued to speak to Catherine Campbell, who was not present at the time, warning her that although she had a stick in her hand she would not be permitted to force it into her mouth, before going on to quote scripture from the Bible and state that Campbell would never take her life from her. Her fits continued for several more days, during which it was on occasion necessary to hold her down from fear she might physically climb the walls, and she continued to give names of those who were invisibly tormenting her.

Eventually, they stopped, and after a week of being in seemingly good health, Christian returned home on the 8th December, yet as before, the seizures soon returned, this time with her saying the Devil had shown himself to her. Her body began to contort horribly during the seizures, yet between them, she again seemed to be healthy. On 17th December, during a seizure, she again began to call out names, stating these people were present and harming her. She reached out and claimed to have got hold of one by his jacket to try to stop him. After the seizure, she opened her hand to reveal a piece of red, torn cloth.

This continued into January when the suggestion was made to bring Agnes Naismith to see Christian. Agnes was the woman who had spoken to her just before this all started and who was named during the seizures as a main tormenter. When Agnes visited, she prayed for the young girl, and she later reported that she was never tormented by her during her seizures again. A request was made for Catherine Campbell to do the same, in the hope that it would bring an end to the seizures, but she refused, with some accounts stating that she told the family she hoped the devil would never let her get better for what she had done. It was at this point it was decided to report the matter to the authorities, and Catherine was imprisoned.

While Catherine was held in the tollbooth, several observations were made. When she was jailed, it was claimed a ball of multi-coloured hair was found in her pocket, which was thrown onto the fire. After this, Christian stopped producing balls of hair from her mouth. It was also noted that during any seizures, Christian rarely claimed that Catherine was tormenting her, and on the occasions she did, it was found that these were the times that Catherine had been allowed out of her jail, for example, to attend church. Christian's fits did however continue, and she continued to call out other names and started to react violently to the touch of her parents during these sessions, as though she was being stabbed.

On 11th January, her fits took another turn. Rather than lying down during them, she began to walk out of the house and to the gates, which were closed. Some of those who observed felt she was not walking, but was instead floating. This continued for a number of days, each time with her being carried back to her bed where, after a short time, she would recover. She told her parents that between six and ten people were visiting her, and trying to carry her away from the house, or out to the courtyard where they wanted to drown her in the well. No doubt terrified, the decision was made to seek the help of the Church, and two ministers were appointed to spend time with the family and observe Christian.

Over the next few weeks, they would witness the fits, initially praying for her only to be met with laughter. Christian began to be drawn to the basement during her seizures, stating she was being drawn downwards towards the Devil, and she continued to name those who were tormenting her. On both 16th and 17th January, she produced a number of pins from her mouth which she claimed had been forcibly put there by one of her invisible tormentors. Then on 21st January her condition once again seemed to change, with her having violent struggles during her seizures, claiming that she was being attacked by cats, ravens, and owls. On one occasion she stated after a fit that she had heard her tormentors tell her that the Devil had agreed if they could get her to the hall window, then he could get her to the well and drown her, and all would believe she had taken her own life. Later the same day, during a seizure, she was found trying to get out of that very window. Attempts by the ministers to pray or read scripture during her seizures began to get violent reactions from her.

With there seemingly being no end to their daughter's suffering, the family sought further help from the authorities, and on 4th February, those named as her tormentors began to be taken in for questioning. Christian's seizures continued, with her claiming that those who had been taken in for interrogation were visiting her during their questioning trying to make her stop, and that she was receiving further threats. On several further occasions, she also produced mouthfuls of pins, which she claimed had been forced into her mouth by her tormentors, and she began to find a number of strange items hidden around the house, which were believed to have been placed there to give her tormentors power over her. Meanwhile, the ministers continued to try to help, and on 28th March, her seizures stopped and she made a full recovery. While she went on to live a long and happy life as a successful businesswoman working in the Paisley thread industry and marrying a loving husband, those she accused were not so fortunate.

Throughout the months, she had named a total of 35 people who she claimed were tormenting her. Eventually, the two main accused Catherine Campbell and Agnes Naismith, along with five others, Margaret Laing, James Lindsay, Thomas Lindsay, John Reid, and Margaret Fulton were charged and put on trial for using witchcraft to inflict illness on Christian Shaw. All denied the charges, but once inside the 'system' facing the power of the Church and town authorities, along with the usual torture used as part of the interrogation process, it was inevitable that all were to be found guilty and sentenced to death.

John Reid committed suicide by hanging himself in the jail prior to the sentence being carried out, and on 10th June, the remaining six were taken to Gallow Green, just of Castle Street, where there were first hung, then burned at the stake. While it was not unusual for a convicted witch to be strangled before being burned, hanging was unusual in Scotland, but it is perhaps a combination of there being six convicts to execute, and wanting to make a spectacle of the event as a warning to others, that hanging was chosen. According to some reports, it was not however successful, and several were still alive when they were cut down from the gallows and taken to the waiting fires, leading to one of the executioners borrowing a walking stick from an onlooker, to push one of the victims back into the flames as they tried to claw their way out.

Although reports state all six were executed, there is some debate over the fate of the brothers, Thomas and James Lindsay, who were just 11 and 14 years old. Some reports describe how they were garrotted rather than being hung, and they clutched each other as their young lives were drained from them, whereas later reports state they escaped execution on the day, although their fate was not known. Never the less, this was to be the last mass execution for witchcraft in Western Europe. Neither Catherine Campbell nor Agnes Naismith were willing to go to their deaths quietly. Catherine is said to have had to be carried to the gallows, shouting out that her accusers would face the wrath of both God and the Devil, while Agnes cursed everyone present and their descendants.

The ashes of the accused were buried at the crossroad of Maxwellton Street and George Street, a common place to bury anyone executed as the belief was if the spirit did rise, it would not know which way to go to reach those it sought vengeance against. A horseshoe was placed above the burial spot, yet every misfortune that befalls Paisley is attributed to the Witches Curse. During roadworks in the 1960s, the horseshoe was removed from the site, and the town fell into a period of decline. It has since been returned, forming a more significant memorial for those burned as witches.

Horseshoe memorial at Maxwellton Cross (please be aware of the heavy traffic if you decide to visit, it's in the middle of one of Paisley's busiest junctions) Credit: Paisley Scotland/Flickr/Licenced under CC 2.0 Generic/Adapted to Greyscale by Beul Aithris Publishing from colour

The Maggie Wall Monument

The best-known witch memorial is dedicated to Maggie Wall and situated close to the village of Dunning, but it is also the most mysterious, as no one knows who Maggie Wall was.

At nearly 20 feet tall, and built from large stones fixed together with iron staples, the monument is probably the most substantial of all of the older memorials. Curiously, it is topped with a cross, something that may seem strange given that the Church was one of the main persecutors during the time of the witch trials. Painted on the memorial are the words 'Maggie Wall Burnt Here 1657 as a Witch'. The size of the monument and information in the inscription might lead an observer to think that the details of the trial were well known, but in reality not only is there no record of Maggie Wall in the witch trials records, there is no record of her living in the parish, and no record of when the monument was built, or by whom! The whole matter is a mystery.

Dunning was no stranger to strong women in the past, and so there are many theories on possible candidates for the real woman behind the name. In the middle of the 17th century, Dunning experienced a period of unrest against the Church. The local minister, the Reverend George Muschet had been deemed unfit to preach following an argument with the Church leaders who had accused him of putting the word of God into question. Muschet was possibly in opposition to the witch persecutions. A group of representatives was sent by the Church hierarchy to discipline, possibly even remove the Reverend from his position, but they did not appreciate just how popular he was with the local community. Upon arrival at Dunning, the men were set upon by a group of over 100 women, The officials were sent running, having lost their cloaks and horses, and receiving a sound beating. The result was not just the women of Dunning being condemned by the Church council, but the whole of the female sex being declared as 'evil'.

Reverend Muschet died in 1663, having been previously replaced by the Reverend Andrew Rollo, with the witch hysteria arriving in Dunning a year before his death. During these trials of 1662, there were six accused witches, Issobell Goold, Agnes Hutstone, Anna Law, Issobell McKendley, Elspeth Reid and Jonet Toyes. The records show that Issobell Goold, Agnes Hutstone and Anna Law were imprisoned with no confession. Issobell McKendley, Elspeth Reid, and Jonet Toyes were however convicted, strangled and burned. Cross referring to the trials, a Jonet Airth is also referred to in the case of Issobell Goold, and she too was sentenced to death.

Those overseeing the trials included James Rollo and Laurence Rollo, relatives of the Reverend Andrew Rollo. Their name also appears as commissioners on other trials in 1662, including Jonet Allan (no details of the outcome), Jonnett Annand (no further details), Jonet Binning (no further details), Elizabeth Crow (no further details), Margaret Crose (executed), Helen Ilson (executed), Jonet Marin (executed), Agnes Ramsay (no further details), Jonet Robe (no further details) and Jonet Young (executed). It is fair to say 1662 was indeed a year of witch madness in the local area with devastating effects on the local community.

Yet despite all of this information, it really brings us no closer to who Maggie Wall was or why, with all of the other unfortunate victims of the witch trials, a monument to her alone was created. Nor does it give any indication on when it was built, or who had it constructed. To build it would have almost certainly incurred considerable costs, and needed permission from the landowners. To add to the mystery, it is located just outside the village, on the main thoroughfare from Dunning, yet not even local hearsay seems to give any clear idea on who built it. It would not be unreasonable to expect that there would be some record of its construction, either in the town records or passed down through generations.

There are many suggestions: some argue that Maggie Wall was one of the ring leaders of the rebellion against the Church in the 17th century and, as a result, was made an example of by the authorities as a warning to others not to oppose them. This theory is plausible, with the punishment faced by Maggie not being documented and the earlier condemnation of women being evil, being interpreted as them being witches. Yet it offers no explanation why such a monument would later be erected for Maggie alone, when the Church showed no remorse for the other townsfolk later accused, tortured and executed for witchcraft.

The biggest clue may lie in the land. The monument is built in the former estate of Duncrub Castle, home of the Rollo family - the same family involved in overseeing the witch trials of 1662, and for earlier replacing the minister. As the head of the local Church, and the main landowners of the area, they were very much in the thick of the misfortune that befell the town. There is even a local rumour that Maggie Wall was a maid at the castle, and fell pregnant to one of the sons. Unfortunately for her, rather than this being a happy time, she was disposed of to hide the evidence and remove any risk or harm to the family name. In these times, when the powerful were responsible for writing the official records, such an act was possible.

If the Rollo family were involved in the monument, this would certainly explain the question of obtaining permission from the landowners. In 2011, author Geoff Holder put forward an argument which is one of the most convincing I have read. He identifies that a map from the 1700s shows a field around the area of the monument named Muggies Walls. He further identified that a map dated 1829 also showed a patch of woodland to be called Maggie Walls Woods. With the monument appearing on maps from 1866, it is fair to theorize it was built at some point between the creation of the 18th-century map, and 1866 when reference to the monument first appeared. Holder presents a case that during the late 18th century, these lands were tenanted to the local schoolmaster, David Balmain. In addition to being a schoolmaster, Balmain was a builder and carried out considerable building work on the land, which may have extended to the construction of the monument, with the consent of the Rollo family as recompense for their ancestors' involvement in the trials.

While this theory gives plausible answers to some of the mystery around the monument, it does not, however, answer others. The words painted on the stones are a clear today as they were in historical photographs, with it being said the inscription is repainted every year, yet no one knows who carries this out. In addition, a wreath is laid annually with a card reading 'In memory of Maggie Wall, burnt by the Church in the name of Christianity'. Again, no one knows who lays the wreath, or the origins of the words written on the card. It may be there is local knowledge that is shared among a select few only. A number of offerings are also regularly placed at the monument, with many children's toys pushed in the gaps between the stones. The reason for children's toys being favoured is not known, there is nothing to suggest the monument is a memorial to a child.

The most widely believed theory is that the monument is in fact dedicated to all of those persecuted for witchcraft in the local area. As noted earlier, the fate of some are not known, and there may have been others not documented, and so to take a name related to the local area to cover all of the accused may seem a more poignant way to remember them all. This does however still leave one the question. The field and the wooded area shown on the maps named after Maggie Wall must have taken the name from someone, and so the mystery remains, who was Maggie Wall?

The Maggie Wall Monument, Dunning

The Witch Stone of Monzie

Although not specifically marked with any inscription, date or plaque, a standing stone on the meandering road leading to Monzie Castle in Perthshire is said to mark the spot where a woman named Kate McNiven was put to death.

Kate's story is quite bizarre, even by the witch trial standards. It is said she worked as a nanny for the Graeme family of Inchbrakie, whose castle stood to the east of Crieff. She built quite a reputation as a herbalist, with many seeking her help and advice in treating all manners of illnesses. This was, however, a practice much frowned upon by the authorities, with the belief that the ill should pray for healing, and being caught producing or using herbal remedies was almost certain to lead to accusations of witchcraft.

It was almost inevitable she would eventually come to the attention of the authorities, and perhaps with some knowledge of what was coming, the Graeme family released her from her duties and she returned to her home town of Kirkton of Monzie. If this was an attempt by the Graemes to save her, is sadly failed as suspicion grew as to the reasons why she was let go by the family, and her reputation soon caught up with her. A story spread that while the Laird of Inchbrakie was hosting a dinner party, he had been tormented by a bee at the dining table. In an attempt to rid himself of the flying nuisance, the

Laird had put down his cutlery to try to swat the bee away, only to find that after he had successfully directed it out of a window, that his cutlery was nowhere to be found. After the party, he discussed the strange incident with his household staff, only for Kate to go and check and return with his fork and knife which were exactly where they should have been. Rumours spread that Kate had used witchcraft to turn herself into a bee, and it was her that had pestered the Laird and taken his cutlery, only to return them later, which had resulted in the loss of her employment at the castle.

With this story, evidence of her using herbs to heal and other claims of sorcery being made, Kate's fate was sealed. She is said to have been first taken to the hill known as the Knock of Crieff, where she was rolled down the hill in a barrel, no doubt causing considerable injuries. She was then taken to the grounds of Monzie Castle, where she was burned at the stake. According to the lore, the Laird of Inchbrakie had been unaware of what had happened to his former nanny, nor the allegations connected to his family, until he was returning home when he stumbled across the execution. He attempted to stop the fire being lit, begging the gathered crowd to aid him, but he was unsuccessful. As soon as the fire was lit, Kate bit a blue bead from her necklace and spat it to the Laird, before proceeding to speak. She initially cursed the Laird of Monzie, before cursing the whole town of the

Kirkton of Monzie, and finally told the Laird of Inchbrakie that in thanks for his kindness, as long as his family held the blue bead she had given him within his land, they would prosper.

While it is not my intention to debate the curse in this book, it has aided the story of Kate to live on thanks to being passed down from generation to generation, which is useful as there is no mention of her in the official records. Even the year of her execution is much debated, with the suggestions of 1563, 1643 and even 1715 being put forward, due to mentions that may tie into the story in other writings, or a similar name being referenced in other trial records as the 'witch from Monzie'.

While this may lead many to suspect that the story is completely untrue, the Graeme family records do show that a blue moonstone, which had been set into a ring, was passed down through the generations. In addition there are several places such as Kate McNiven's Crag, Kate McNiven's Well and Kate McNiven's Cave, all of which are near Crieff and, combined with the cross-reference from other trial records mentioned above, it seems Kate was very much a real person but was one of the many for whom sadly records were not kept.

cc-by-sa-2.0 - The Witch's Stone by Ewen Rennie - geograph.org.uk/p/900143

The Monzie Witches Stone

The Witches Stone of Spott

On the roadside in the small hamlet of Spott in East Lothian, a small memorial to the area's dark past sits which, even at around 1 metre high and protected by an iron fence, is easily missed if you do not know it is there. A small memorial plaque beside the stone reads:

Marion Lillie, the Ringwoody Witch was burnt here in 1698
The stone is reputed to stand on the site of the burning of the last witch in the South of Scotland
Near to this site the Birley Tree stood, under whose branches the local Birley Court was held.

While this tiny settlement may not be the most obvious place to associate with witch trials, the location of around ten miles from North Berwick resulted in it being drawn into the frenzy from the notorious North Berwick Witch Trials, and while the stone may be dedicated to Marian Lillie, she was the last of a long list of accused witches.

Most of the trials report there was not enough information to secure a conviction. However, it was not uncommon in these days to hold an accused in prison in the hope that further evidence, no matter how small or seemingly impossible that may be, would emerge that would allow the accusation to proceed to trial. One such case was that of Isobel Young, who faced trial in February 1629. To support the suspicions, it was alleged that some 29 years earlier she had stopped at a man's house, presumably a fisherman, as it is said she spoiled his herring fishing. That, along with claims she had met with the Devil at Doune Hill, Spott, sent her to the flames, with the only blessing being she was strangled to death before the fire was lit.

Marion Lillie's case was much like so many, an unpopular woman who made the unfortunate mistake of standing out from the crowd. There is a clue as to her appearance in her being known as the Ringwoody Witch, as Ringwoody in old Scots would mean thin and boney. This would suggest people were already uncomfortable with her purely due to the way she looked. Whether it was simply her personality or resentment from her of being shunned by the townsfolk, it is said that Marion was not afraid to speak her mind and had a sharp tongue, which ultimately was her downfall.

The records are unclear, however, it is written that while one of her neighbours was looking forward to Mrs. Gamp and the Caudle-Cup, Marian, a passionate tongued old dame, handled her so roughly that Mrs. Gamp and the Caudle-Cup were forestalled. This is an example of trying to decipher exactly what it is said she did! The reference to Mrs. Gamp, made better known by Charles Dickens, would refer to a midwife, and the Caudle-Cup was a two-handled cup used during the 17th century, in which a mix of warm ale or wine, mixed with bread, eggs, sugar, and spices, was given to a woman after giving birth to aid in rebuilding her strength. It is apparent her neighbour was therefore pregnant. The reference to handling her roughly is unlikely to mean a physical assault - it should be remembered that Marion was frail and elderly - but perhaps means a verbal assault, and the forestalling of the Caudle-Cup suggests that the neighbour sadly suffered a miscarriage. Of course there is no clear evidence that this sad event was as a direct result of her altercation with Marian, however, that would be irrelevant when it came to having an opportunity to rid the local community of this unpopular resident.

As with other such stones, the date when it was put in place, or who was responsible and their reasons for doing so are unknown, however, it is documented in writings from 1845, which suggested that the that the stone may have been in place as early as 1705, and that it was sat close to the manse (which no longer stands).

Although the memorial plaque states the Ringwoody Witch was the last to be burnt in Southern Scotland, brothers George and Lachlan Rattray were accused and found guilty of the crimes of witchcraft and sorcery in 1705 and put to death on top of Spott Loan. Whether the stone predates this, or whether they were not deemed to being witches due to being male is not known. The Witches Stone of Spott is however generally accepted to commemorate all of those who lost their life at Spott.

The Witches Stone, Spott

The Witches Maze, Tullibole Castle, Perthshire

Within the grounds of Tullibole Castle, a maze is dedicated in memory of the 11 victims who died under accusations of witchcraft in the village of the Crook of Devon, which the castle sits beside.

It was in 1662 when the witch-mania struck this small village, with claims that there were covens of witches living within the unsuspecting townsfolk. During this time, the court is reported to have sat no less than five times, most likely at Tullibole Castle, as the trials were overseen by William Halliday, and his son John, the owners of the castle. In total 13 people were accused, one male and twelve females. One, Agnes Pittendreich, escaped the death sentence due to being pregnant at the time of the trial, and there are no records of the fate of another, Margaret Hoggin, who avoided conviction despite the evidence being equally reliable as that which saw others condemned to death.

The first accused were Agnes Murie, Bessie Henderson, and Isabella Rutherford, who faced trial on 3ʳᵈ April 1662. Although there are records existing, they are not complete and the exact reason for their conviction is not clear, despite the trial being described as a long and close investigation, resulting in unanimous convictions, with the sentence being that they were to be strangled to death by the executioner, William Donaldson, before their bodies were to be burned to ashes.

The second trial came just a few weeks later and was based on information gathered in the first trial. As was common, once accused the women had been asked to name their accomplices in their evil work, which resulted in the arrest of Robert Wilson, Bessie Neil, Margaret Litster, Janet Paton, and Agnes Brugh. Having already been named by accused witches of being present with them during their meeting with Satan, their fate was more or less sealed, and on 24th April, they too were executed in the same manner by the same executioner. It was during this trial that the name Agnes Pittendreich was mentioned, having been accused by Margaret Litster in her confession of meeting with Satan, along with other women, at a hill known as Gibson's Craig. As mentioned earlier, she was however released when it was found she was pregnant, but on an order that she should return to the court within 15 days of being called upon to answer the charges against her, or face death.

Next to face trial were Margaret Hoggin and Janet Paton. Information on their charges are scant, yet both are described as being widows, with Margaret being said to be 79 years of age, and so it may have been a simple attempt to rid the town of old women. While Margaret was released due to her age, Janet, who was reported to be just slightly younger, was not so lucky and met the same fate as the others. On 5th May, the same day of her conviction, she was executed at the hands of Alexander Abernethie.

A brief lull in the frenzied trials followed, with it being said factions of the witches covens had fled, yet by 21st July, two had been captured. Janet Brugh and Christian Grieve both faced the accusations of witchcraft yet only Janet was convicted, with Thomas Gibson being named as the executioner. While Christian may have beaten the odds and gone free on this occasion, she was again accused in October of the same year, and convicted by the same jury, before being put to death on 13th October.

There are several theories on what started these trials, yet the conclusion is, as, with so many of the trials, it was simple neighbour disputes or individuals who were willing to speak their mind and so drew attention to themselves. Once the trial process began, under cruel and harsh treatment, sleep deprivation and likely torture, those accused began to confess to meetings with Satan, no doubt suggested to them by their interrogators, and in naming others who were also guilty, and so it escalated. The Church is particularly criticised in later writings about the trials for being overzealous in their pursuit of convictions, no matter how weak the available evidence was.

In 2012, Lord Moncrieff, the current owner of Tullibole Castle, opened the maze which he had commissioned to commemorate those who lost their lives in the 1662 trials, with a pillar bearing their names lying at the centre. Work had in fact started in 2003, with the completed maze consisting of around 2000 beech trees. Lord Moncrieff's aim with the maze was not just to have a memorial for the accused witches, but also to encourage visitors to think about the time of the trials, rather than just apply modern-day logic to what were once very real beliefs and fears.

Tullibole Castle

The Orkney Memorial Plaque

The fear of witchcraft arrived on the island of Orkney at the same time and under similar suspicions to the North Berwick trials.

In 1594, Patrick Stewart succeeded his father, Robert, as the Earl of Orkney, and soon after found poison in the pockets of one of his brother John's servants. Fearing that there was a plot to kill him, he ordered that both his brother and his servant, Thomas Paplay, be tried for attempted murder. Patrick was the cousin of King James VI and as children, they had been close, and it seems he followed the actions of the King in the Berwick Witch trials, and opted to obtain a confession by torture, on the basis witchcraft was a plausible explanation for the attempt on his life.

Paplay suffered horrifically, undergoing the agony of a device known as the Cashiclaws, an iron frame that fitted around the legs and was slowly heated until the metal burned into the skin. He also endured having his feet crushed in the 'booties' and being flogged with rope, ripping off his skin. Eventually, he confessed and named Alison Balfour, a local lady described as a notorious witch, as his accomplice. Thomas was sentenced to be burned at the stake and, despite withdrawing his confession a short time before his execution, Alison was arrested and taken in for interrogation.

By all accounts, Alison was a remarkably strong woman, undergoing the same treatment as Thomas, yet refusing to admit to crimes she did not commit. Determined to get a confession, her family consisting of her elderly husband, son and young daughter were arrested and also underwent torture while she was forced to watch. Her husband had what was said to be a 50 stone weight placed on his chest to slowly crush him, while her son had his feet crushed in the booties, suffering a total of 57 strikes of the mallet driving stakes into the device, however, it was her daughter suffering the agony of the piniwinkies, a form of thumb screw, that finally broke her and she too confessed to plotting to kill the Earl.

As with Thomas, she was sentenced to death by burning, and she too withdrew her confession moments before, describing the torture that she and her family had suffered, yet the execution went ahead, with Alison being the first of many who would be accused of and executed for witchcraft. John Stewart himself was later accused of consulting with a witch, an act that under the 1563 Witchcraft Act was punishable by death, yet no doubt due to his status, he was acquitted. The evidence he had presented blaming Alison was also thrown out due to it being obtained under torture, yet it was sadly too late for her.

Other notable trials in Orkney include that of Elspeth Reoch and Janet Forsyth. Elspeth faced trial in 1616, after suspicion fell on her for picking herbs. Not a great crime by today's standards, but enough to draw the attention of the authorities in the 17th century. It was, however, Elspeth being overheard muttering a few words every time she knelt down to pick the plants that raised the most concern to the locals, as Elspeth was known to be mute.

Once she was taken in for questioning, her story came out. Elspeth had been born in Caithness, on the northeast tip of mainland Scotland, before travelling to the Islands. It seems for much of her life she had been a bit of a drifter, preferring her own company to that of her family. She fell pregnant to an unknown man and it was after the birth of her first child that she lost her speech. By this time, it seems her parents had already passed as her brother is described as being the most senior member of the family while on Orkney.

His treatment of her to try to make her speak again was both cruel and perhaps a sign of what was to come as, very similar to a method to torture an accused witch, he resorted to first beating her before starting to secure a fine rope tightly around her head, which would cause excruciating pain. Why he went to this effort to make her speak is unknown. Perhaps he was trying to make her reveal the identity of the baby's father, yet Janet withstood all of the punishment he could deliver, and remained silent. Running out of options, he started to take her to church to pray for her speech to come back, but this too failed and eventually Elspeth returned to her days of wandering from town to town.

By the time of her arrest, Elspeth had a second child, again with the father being unknown. That would be enough to make her stand out from the crowd, and when adding her roaming lifestyle, fondness for picking herbs and being unable to speak yet being overheard muttering a few words when picking her herbs, it was pretty much inevitable that she would find herself with an accusation of witchcraft hanging over her.

In her confession, Elspeth is said to have claimed that she had been involved with the Faeries since the age of 12. It is important to remember that in Scottish folklore, Faeries are not the friendly, winged variety popular today, but were mischievous spirits, said to be too good to go to Hell, but too evil to go to Heaven, and so remained earthbound. They are also said to have held all the understanding of herbal remedies, and it was they that Elspeth claimed taught her how to treat ailments, with instructions to always kneel on her right knee before picking the herb between her thumb and middle finger, while reciting the charm for the magic she sought, such as to cure a disease.

Despite claiming to have no speech, it was said Elspeth made a living from using her ability of Second Sight to foretell the future, an ability also given to her by the Faerie Folks. She is claimed to have said that while visiting a loch one day, two men appeared to her, one wearing green tartan with the other dressed totally in black. They taught her how to use Second Sight by roasting an egg, washing her hands in the steam that came from it, before rubbing her eyes with her hands. Two years later, while she was aiding in the delivery of a baby, the man dressed in black re-appeared to her, and it was he who was the father of her second baby and who was responsible for taking her speech, which she had traded for the power of Second Sight. The courts ruled that this man wearing black was, in fact, the Devil and the other man had been a Faerie. She was found guilty of using Second Sight and herbal remedies and, on 2nd March 1616, poor Elspeth was first strangled to death, before her body was burned on a fire.

Another noteworthy tale from Orkney is that of the Westray Storm Witch, Janet Forsyth. Janet lived on the island of Westray, one of the smallest inhabited islands in the Orkney Isles. Suspicion first fell on Janet when she had an unusual dream, in which she saw her boyfriend, Ben Garrioch, drown at sea. Knowing he was due to go on a fishing trip the following day, she rushed to beg him not to go, but he just laughed her warning off. Later that day the island was shrouded in a thick fog, and the boat carrying Ben and the other men never returned.

Janet was heartbroken, her grief no doubt compounded by the fact that she had not been able to persuade Ben not to go, and as a result, she became reclusive. However, the loss of several young men in a small island community had dire effects, and with Janet's warnings being overheard by others who were now looking for someone to blame for the tragedy, it wasn't long before they were re-interpreted as a threat made to the fishermen, and rumours started that Janet had created the weather conditions that resulted in the loss of the boat and crew.

Janet's self-imposed isolation only served to aid the local gossip and she found herself being blamed every time a storm hit the island. On one occasion, a ship was spotted in trouble just off the coast during a storm. Janet begged the watching townsfolk to help, but she was ignored, partly through fear and partly through ignorance. So Janet decided to take the matter into her own hands, and took her own small boat out on the stormy seas and managed to guide the ship to the safety of a sheltered bay.

Any hopes she had that such an act of bravery may change the local opinion on her were soon dashed, and the islanders decided that it would be impossible for a woman to face such a severe storm and survive, and so the only way she could have achieved what she had, was through the use of witchcraft.

Janet was taken to Kirkwall on the mainland of Orkney to face trial for witchcraft, and it was there in the principal town of the island network that she once again set eyes upon Ben Garrioch. It transpired that he and his fellow fishermen had not been lost at sea as feared, but instead had been press-ganged into joining the Navy. She was imprisoned at St Magnus Cathedral, but the following morning her cell was found to be empty, with it being suspected that Garrioch had aided her escape.

She did, however, end up back on Westray, and it didn't take long for the authorities to once again catch up with her. She was accused, amongst other things, of causing illness in some cattle by taking drops of their blood and putting it into a fire on Halloween, and also of causing a crop of barley in a field owned by Robert Reid and another owned by Michael Reid (probably brothers) to fail, and for several years she would either allow the crop to grow to harvert or fail entirely, depending on her mood towards the men. On 11th November 1629, Janet was executed in the traditional style of being strangled at the stake, with her body then being burned.

In total, it is thought at least 19 women and one man were accused of witchcraft in Orkney, and on 9th March 2019, a monument to them was unveiled in Kirkwall at Gallow Ha', the place where the victims lost their lives.

*Orkney memorial after completion. Credit:
Mark Woodford-Dean*

Orkney memorial in situ. Credit Mark Woodford-Dean

The Forfar Witch Memorial

The town of Forfar in the county of Angus is perhaps best known for the Forfar Bridie, the semi-circled shaped pie known to most in Scotland that is said to have been first made in the town in the 1850s, however, the town has a darker past that has led it to, on occasion, be referred to as Scotland's Salem.

The first witch trials in Forfar were in 1568 when Catherine Campbell, Cristeane Jak, and Issobell Sutye all faced charges of using witchcraft. However, it was in 1661 that something of a witch frenzy struck Forfar, triggered by some accounts to be due to a simple argument between a local lady named Isobell Shyrie and one of the town officials. Rumours started that Isobell had cursed the official, resulting in her being taken in for trial under the charge of using witchcraft. The records show that she did confess to her alleged offence, yet rather than being sent to the flames, another trial was set, with it being noted no torture was to be used.

This may be due to her naming other women in the town as accomplices as, just a few weeks later, Helen Cothall, Helen Guthrie and Elspeth Alexander were charged, yet this did not save Isobell, who confessed to mixing a potion to try to kill the town Baillie and she was strangled and burned at the stake. Helen Gurthie is noted in numerous records as being notorious for becoming drunk and causing trouble in the town, it may be that the authorities specifically wanted her named so they had reasons to put her to trial, however, if this was the case, I suspect the authorities did not know what they had let themselves in for.

Throughout the trials, the women were kept in horrific conditions, being deprived of any daylight, and with orders for the guards to visit them every three hours to ensure they were not allowed to sleep. The services of the notorious witch-pricker, John Kincaid, were also employed at one point, and he did so well at obtaining the evidence and confessions, he was made a Freeman of the Burgh. It is therefore apparent that some of the most horrendous torture was used, which may explain some of the confessions made.

Helen Guthrie was the first to confess. As with so many of the witch trials, such a confession may have been to end the brutal treatment of the accused. Although it is also recorded that Helen's young daughter, Jonet Howet, was also arrested and some believe that Helen made her first confession, and then subsequent confessions, to keep the attention on her and away from her daughter. If this was her intention, it worked as Jonet survived the 1661 trials, although sadly the suspicions and tall tales caught up with her again in 1666 when she was once again arrested for the crime of witchcraft, although her fate is not documented.

Fortunately, the records of the accused confessions survived, and so relatively detailed accounts can be given. Helen Guthrie is noted in these records to have been a 'Very Drunkensome woman' and a 'curser and of a very wicked life'. She confessed to being a witch, saying she learnt her craft from a woman named Joanet Galloway 14 years before her trial, and that she had the ability to identify any witch in Scotland, thanks a three bloody papers that were given to her by Joanet, which she refused to hand over and stated that she would take to the fire with her.

She also confessed to have the ability to curse people, with her wishes taking effect within just 24 hours, to be able to identify curses from other witches and that, while imprisoned, the Devil had visited her and tried to carry her away, an act that would have been successful had three watchmen not seen her float the feet above the ground and intervene by striking the invisible force with their swords. Her final documented confession was simply to say that she had many other things still to confess, and would do so before she went to the fire. Of everything she claimed she had done, or could do, it was the ability to identify other witches that perhaps caught the interest of the authorities the most, and she did indeed go on to name others, which kept the trials going.

Helen later did go on to confess other crimes, just as she had promised. She said that when her half sister, Margaret, was around six or seven years old, she killed Margaret by stroking her shoulder and, by doing so, poisoning her blood, resulting in their mother cursing Helen for the rest of her life.

She further confessed that three years prior to her arrest, she had met with the Devil in Forfar Churchyard, where she and a number of others, who she went on to name, danced with the Devil, an act that she repeated the following year, terrifying some locals who saw it. The nature of the confessions then took a more sinister twist with Helen claiming that after a third such meeting with the Devil and the rest of her Coven, they returned to John Bennyes house to drink ale and dine.

She went on to say that some of the Coven had located the body of a recently deceased unbaptised child while at the churchyard, and that they had taken several parts of the body, which they cooked in a pie for them all to eat. She continued to state that her coven had pulled down a vital bridge in the area and that they had later caused a ship to sink in the bay. This is not a full list of Helen's confessions but it does cover the main ones which led these trials to become quite notorious. Throughout her confessions, she continued to provide further names that she alleged were also witches and in total, including Helen herself, 14 men and women were executed or exiled, largely down to Helen's confessions.

In 2010, a local couple named in the press as Mark and Marie Carshley, commissioned a sculptor to make a memorial stone for the 22 people who died in Forfar throughout the centuries on charges of witchcraft. The stone had 22 dots on it to symbolise the victims, and the words 'Forfar Witches' and 'Just People' as a poignant reminder that anyone could have found themselves facing accusation and almost certain death in these times. The stone stands at the bottom of their garden alongside Forfar Loch.

Forfar Memorial. Credit: The Travelling Witch

The Last Witch to Burn

In the garden of a private home in the Highland town of Dornoch, a simple stone commemorates the final execution on the charge of Witchcraft in Scotland.

The records indicate that Dornoch had largely avoided the hysteria of the witch trials throughout the 16th and 17th centuries, but in the 18th century, suspicions fell upon a local woman named Janet Horne. Although no official records remain of Janet's story, it is known, in part, thanks to the writings of Captain William Burt, an author and rent collector for the British Government. After the 1715 Jacobite uprising, Burt was sent to Scotland to aid with the collections of rents and with the arrangements for the construction of military roads, which were overseen by General Wade.

Burt wrote a series of letters about his experiences in Northern Scotland, which were later published in 1754 under the title of *Letters from a Gentleman in the North of Scotland to his Friend in London*. Included within the letters are references to his surprise that while most of Britain now saw the belief in witchcraft as nothing but nonsense, there was still a strong and genuine fear in the North of Scotland. He also recalls, all-be-it briefly, the story of Janet.

From what is known, Janet once held a rather prestigious role as a Lady's maid, which allowed her to travel all around Europe with the family which she served, meaning she may well have been very knowledgeable in different cultures and beliefs. That alone may have been enough to cast suspicion on her within small, localised communities, especially if she was able to speak even a few words of a different language.

When she returned to Scotland, she settled in the Sutherland region where she married and had a daughter. Little is known about her life, or what happened to her husband, but it is known at the time of her accusation she was living with her daughter in a small village in the Loth region of Sutherland. Her daughter is said to have deformed hands and feet, with some accounts saying she had suffered burn injuries as a child, while other accounts say they were simple birth defects.

This again would add to any suspicion about Janet, yet it was not until she began to become confused and muddled in her old age, that her neighbours finally decided to raise their concerns. Both Janet and her daughter were taken to the tollbooth in Dornoch where the incoherent ramblings of Janet resulted in an accusation of witchcraft. They were accused of numerous misdemeanours, including the bewitching of animals, and the deformity in the hands and feet of Janet's daughter were likened to be hooves, with it being said Janet turned her daughter into a pony, which the Devil had shod, resulting in the injuries. It was further claimed that Janet continued to turn her daughter into a pony to ride to her secret meetings with the Devil.

Suffering from what would now be recognised as dementia, Janet had no reply to the accusations. During the trial, she was asked to recite the Lords Prayer, yet she made a mistake in recalling the first line which was seen as conclusive proof she was under the control of Satan. Seemingly keen to put the matter to rest, they were swiftly convicted, and sentenced to be executed the following day. Overnight, Janet's daughter managed to escape, yet in her confused state, and no doubt much to her daughter's despair, Janet did not understand what was happening and remained at the tollbooth.

Her execution was horrific. It is said she was stripped naked before being tarred and feathered and paraded through the town to the execution spot, where she was burned alive in a barrel of oil. The only blessing was that, right up until the oil was lit, it seems Janet had no idea what her fate was, with an account from 1819 telling that when she arrived at the waiting fire, she warmed herself against it commenting that it was a 'braw fire'.

The site of Janet's execution was originally outside the town boundary before a small settlement known as Little Town was built beside it, which was later absorbed into the growing town of Dornoch. It is marked by a simple stone bearing the date, 1722. This is in fact wrong, with the year of Janet's execution being 1727. Who put the stone in place, or their motives behind it are unknown, although it has been marked on maps as far back as the mid-1800s.

This was not, however, Dornoch's only 'claim to fame' connected to the witch trials. Although the Scottish Witchcraft Act of 1563 was finally repealed in 1735, it seems the belief remained. In 1738, a local man named Donald MacKay took matters into his own hands and killed a woman he suspected of witchcraft. While his claims that she had turned into a hare before he killed her may have been widely accepted just a few decades earlier, the authorities saw differently and he was hung at Gallows Hill for the crime of Murdering a Witch.

The Dornoch Witch Stone

A National Monument?

Throughout this book, I have covered most of the acknowledged witch memorials in Scotland, yet there are more stones and sites associated with the witch trials. These sad times are becoming increasingly recognised as something that should be remembered.

In Prestonpans, after a long campaign, a formal pardon and acknowledgement of the innocence of the 81 people who died on the charge of witchcraft in the town was granted and a modern sculpture depicting a woman was added to a new housing estate in their memory.

There are also currently campaigns ongoing for a memorial in Irvine, particularly for Margaret Barclay who, following an argument with her in-laws was accused of cursing her brother-in-law and his wife. After suffering unbearable torture, she confessed and was strangled and then burnt in 1618, but not before being forced to name others who were also accused and tortured.

Whilst the individual memorials to specific cases or areas should be encouraged, there is also a growing campaign for a national monument, to commemorate all of those who died on nothing other than false charges. This is something that I wholeheartedly support, and the Facebook pages 'Fife Witches Remembered' and 'A Memorial for Scotland's Accused Witches' are leading the way. Fife has been suggested due to the high numbers of victims in the county, and the Beamer Beacon has been identified as a potential monument. The beacon is a small lighthouse, originally constructed in 1844 on the Beamer Rock in the Firth of Forth, but was later dismantled in 2011 to make way for the new road bridge being constructed across the river. The stonework has been in storage since and is generally considered to be suitable to be re-modelled as a memorial, with ideas for the design being considered.

A suitable site is currently being sought, yet some feel the subject matter of the proposed monument to still be controversial, and there are many considerations that need to be taken into account, including the infrastructure to be able to deal with the potential number of visitors. For example, it is estimated that approximately 60,000 people visit the Witch House in Salem, Massachusetts in the month of October alone. Although it would take time for any Scottish Memorial to see such numbers, the potential growth of the tourist industry around the memorial is an important factor to be allowed for in the decision making.

With a National Apology to those accused of witchcraft and their families also being sought, I would strongly urge anyone reading this book to join the Facebook pages mentioned to help make the National Monument a reality.

Other titles by Gregor Stewart

Haunted Kirkcaldy (2014 The History Press)

Supernatural St Andrews (2015 Independent)

Glasgow Ghost Stories (2016 Bradwell Books)

Secret St Andrews (2016 Amberley Publishing)

Ghosts of Scotland (2017 Beul Aithris Publishing)

Dundee at Work: People and Industries Through the Years (2017 Amberley Publishing)

St Andrews Pubs (2017 Amberley Publishing)

Secret Dumfermline (2018 Amberley Publishing)

Secret Inverness (2018 Amberley Publishing)

Secret Dundee (2018 Amberley Publishing)

Secret Stirling (2019 Amberley Publishing)

Edinburgh's Military History (2019 Amberley Publishing)

Stirling's Military History (2020 Amberley Publishing)

As G Stewart

Haunted Scottish Castles and Houses

Scottish Ghosts and Witches

Scotland's Hidden Hauntings

Tales of The Supernatural

Gateway Manor

Rise of the Witch

A Troll Bridge

A Kindred Friendship

The Demon Blade

Rebirth of the Witch

The Witch Hunter Series Omnibus

Diary Of An Ordinary Man: What Would You Do If The Zombies Attacked

Zombie Colony Part One: Outbreak

Backseat Driver

Like A 70s Horror Movie

The Diner

Printed in Great Britain
by Amazon

75766161R00061